CONTENTS

Materials List

Unless stated otherwise, assume one item (or set) per student.

Number Sense
24 square tiles
36 counters (or beans)
newspapers
Base 10 blocks (optional)
calculators (optional)

Computation
counting manipulatives (optional)
coins (optional)

Word Problems
calculators (optional)
counting manipulatives (optional)

Geometry
ruler
3 toothpicks
one-inch graph paper
square sheet of paper
4 square tiles

Measurement
ruler (inch and centimeter)
yardstick
coins (optional)
meter stick (optional)
9 cubes

Probability
decks of cards (1 for each pair of students)
a pair of number cubes
2 pennies
various colored blocks or tiles
sugar cube
felt tip marker
various manipulatives (student choice)

Graphing and Statistics
colored pencil
crayons
graph paper
grocery store advertisements
reading book

Connections
4 different colors of paper
scissors
9 toothpicks
39 beans (or counters)
calculators (optional)
coins (optional)

MATH WARM-UPS

For Grades 2 and 3

Karen M. Higgins

Diane Price-Stone

Scott McFadden

DALE SEYMOUR PUBLICATIONS®

DEDICATION

We would like to dedicate this book to Scott McFadden, a beloved colleague, friend, and mentor. Without his initial work and inspiration, this book would not have been written. He is dearly loved and missed.

Royalties from the sale of the book will go to the Oscar Schaaf and Scott McFadden Scholarship Fund. The funds are used to further teachers' professional growth in the teaching of mathematics.

Karen M. Higgins and Diane Price-Stone

Project Editor: Joan Gideon
Production and Manufacturing Coordinator: Leanne Collins
Illustrative Art: Corbin Hillam
Technical Art: Carl Yoshihara
Cover Design: Rachel Gage
Text Design: Francesca Angelesco

Published by Dale Seymour Publications®, an imprint of Addison Wesley Longman, Inc.

    Dale Seymour Publications
    10 Bank Street
    White Plains, New York, NY 10602
    Customer Service: 800-872-1100

Order Number DS21811

ISBN 1-57232-283-7

This product is printed
on recycled paper

**DALE
SEYMOUR
PUBLICATIONS®**

2 3 4 5 6 7 8 9 10 11 12 13-ML-02 01 00 99 98

INTRODUCTION

Math Warm-Ups for Grades 2 and 3 contains 108 Warm-Up lessons, which can set the stage for math time and give you a chance to review math concepts with your students. Each Warm-Up will take about ten minutes to complete. Most Warm-Ups end with an open-ended extension problem for students who have completed the rest of the lesson. Not all students are expected to complete the entire Warm-Up. At the end of ten minutes, you can call time and discuss the questions students have finished.

What are some special Warm-Up features?

Broad Range of Content Consistent with modern curriculum standards, these activities cover a broad range of content organized by these eight strands.

Number Sense
Computation
Word Problems
Geometry
Measurement
Probability
Graphing and Statistics
Connections

Concept and Vocabulary Development Although much of the content of the Warm-Ups is review, some exercises are designed to develop specific concepts and vocabulary. You will probably need to provide extended concept development for some topics or introduce vocabulary relevant to a particular strand.

Communication and Reasoning Students are provided many opportunities to create their own problems and share their mathematical thinking. Since most primary teachers encourage students to share their ideas and to justify their answers and solution processes, the Warm-Ups are written to stimulate such discussion by frequent use of the terms *neighbor* and *friend*. *Neighbor* is used to prompt students to discuss problems with those seated most closely to them. *Friend* is used later on in the lessons to encourage students to seek out and share their ideas with others who have reached the open-ended questions at the end of the Warm-Up.

Problem Solving Problem solving is a central focus of all Warm-Up lessons. In some cases, specific strategies, such as looking for patterns, are highlighted. In most lessons the problems become progressively more difficult, culminating in an open-ended problem, to make the Warm-Ups developmentally appropriate for a wide range of student abilities. Students should be encouraged to try the more challenging problems, but not all students are expected to complete all problems.

Appropriate Computation Mental computation, estimation, and calculator use should all be encouraged. Even though the Warm-Ups can be completed without calculators, if they are available, students should be allowed to use them if they choose.

Teacher Commentary The beginning of the Teacher Commentary contains suggestions for recording Warm-Up solutions. Answers are then provided for each Warm-Up. If special directions are needed for a particular lesson, you will be alerted by the symbol ☑ for "check commentary" in the upper right-hand corner of that Warm-Up. When a Warm-Up contains sentences that may be hard for second graders to read, the Teacher Commentary will suggest you read these to your students. Sometimes you may have to model and discuss the problem before students can begin. Suggestions on how to do this are also contained in the Teacher Commentary. Many open-ended problems have a variety of answers. In these instances, the Teacher Commentary will indicate that "answers will vary."

Materials List In a few instances, special materials will be needed for the Warm-Up lesson. If this is the case, the symbol Ⓜ will be in the upper right-hand corner of the page to alert you. A list of materials you will need is on page iv. The materials needed to complete all the Warm-Up lessons are minimal.

What level do the Warm-Ups address?

- The Warm-Ups were created for students in grades 2 and 3. However, they have been successfully used with advanced first graders and with students in higher grades. Some of them can be used to assess the understanding of older students on topics, such as probability, that may be new to them.
- Because many of the problems are open-ended, Warm-Ups can be used effectively with a classroom of students who have a wide range of ability. For less advanced students, teachers may choose to simplify some of the exercises or even allow more time for the problems. Some of the problems may require a reading level beyond a student's ability. If this is the case, you can read the problems to the class or team up students with more fluent readers.

How should you use the Warm-Ups?

You may choose to make copies of a Warm-Up for each student or pair of students, or you may make transparencies and read the questions to your students. During the field-testing of the materials, it was discovered that many of the Warm-Ups could easily lead to discussions that could last the entire period. It is important to remember that each classroom is different, and the flexibility in exploring the many uses of this text will benefit from your imagination and creativity. Here are some suggested uses.

- Warm-Ups done at the beginning of mathematics class provide good preparation for the rest of the period's activities.
- Since the Warm-Ups are organized by topic, they can be used to introduce particular lessons on those topics.
- Warm-Ups can be used to review specific concepts or to summarize lessons.
- Warm-Ups reinforce students' skills.
- Warm-Ups can be used as homework assignments.
- The open-ended problems at the end of a Warm-Up give teachers an exceptional opportunity to assess students' comfort levels with number ranges and mathematics concepts.

The Warm-Ups have been successfully field tested with students at Philomath Elementary School in Philomath, Oregon. Tom Stone, Sue Garton, Linda Radetich, Genie Mortenson, Cindy Barrie, Laura Jackson, Amy Thompson, and Patricia Later deserve acknowledgment for their valuable suggestions and cooperation.

WARM-UP 1

Write these numbers from least to greatest.

1. 32, 23, 13   _____, _____, _____
2. 55, 45, 54   _____, _____, _____
3. 922, 292, 229   _____, _____, _____
4. 438, 384, 348   _____, _____, _____
5. 345, 543, 534   _____, _____, _____
6. $\frac{1}{2}$, $\frac{1}{4}$, $\frac{3}{4}$ _____, _____, _____

When you count, what number comes next?

7. 17 _____   14. 49 _____
8. 99 _____   15. 90 _____
9. 33 _____   16. 109 _____
10. 175 _____   17. 560 _____
11. 79 _____   18. 271 _____
12. 415 _____   19. 601 _____
13. 324 _____   20. 438 _____

21. If you have time, write some number problems.
    Have a friend answer them.

1. Put the correct symbol in the space.

    > means is greater than.
    < means is less than.
    = means equals.

    a. 13 _____ 25   f. $1 _____ $0.50

    b. 98 _____ 98   g. 909 _____ 99

    c. 39 _____ 72   h. 67 _____ 65 + 2

    d. 14 + 2 _____ 17   i. 3 groups of 2 _____ 2 groups of 3

    e. 45 – 5 _____ 40   j. 4 groups of 2 _____ 1 group of 8

2. Use the three numbers 3, 9, 6.
    Make the largest number possible. _____

3. Use the three numbers 3, 9, 6.
    Make the smallest number possible. _____

4. Use the three numbers 7, 2, 8.
    Make the largest number possible. _____

5. Use the three numbers 7, 2, 8.
    Make the smallest number possible. _____

6. What number is 10 more than 25? _____

7. What number is 10 less than 37? _____

8. If you have time, make up some problems like these.
    Ask a friend to solve them.

Write the number that comes next when you are counting.
What would it look like if you built it with base-ten blocks?
Draw a picture.

1. 28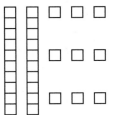

2. 49   _____

3. 56   _____

4. 146   _____

5. 234   _____

6. Think of a number. Write it down.
    Draw a picture of your number as it would look built with
    base-ten blocks.

Look at the first chart. Do you see a number pattern?

1		3		5		7		9	
11	12	13		15		17		19	
21		23		25	26	27		29	
31		33		35		37		39	40
41	42	43	44	45	46	47	48	49	50
51	52	53	54	55	56	57	58	59	60
61	62	63	64	65	66	67	68	69	70

1. What three numbers should be shaded?

2. Shade in the numbers that keep the pattern going.

3. Write down some things you notice about the chart.

Look at the second chart. Do you see a different number pattern?

1	2		4	5		7	8		10
11		13	14	15	16	17		19	20
	22	23		25	26		28	29	
31	32	33	34	35	36	37	38	39	40
41	42	43	44	45	46	47	48	49	50
51	52	53	54	55	56	57	58	59	60
61	62	63	64	65	66	67	68	69	70

4. Find the number that should be shaded on this chart.

5. Shade in numbers that would keep the pattern going.

6. Write down some things you notice about the chart.

WARM-UP 5

Count on from these numbers.

1. 13, _____, _____, _____, _____, _____

2. 47, _____, _____, _____, _____, _____

3. 96, _____, _____, _____, _____, _____

4. 122, _____, _____, _____, _____, _____

5. 204, _____, _____, _____, _____, _____

6. 860, _____, _____, _____, _____, _____

7. Make your own counting-on problems.

Now count backwards.

8. 13, _____, _____, _____, _____, _____

9. 47, _____, _____, _____, _____, _____

10. 96, _____, _____, _____, _____, _____

11. 122, _____, _____, _____, _____, _____

12. 204, _____, _____, _____, _____, _____

13. 860, _____, _____, _____, _____, _____

14. Make your own count-backwards problems.

Which things are easy to count exactly?
Which things are hard to count?
Loop the word *easy* or *hard* for each question.

1.	Number of chairs at a table	easy	hard
2.	Number of pins in a jar	easy	hard
3.	Number of scoops of beans in a jar	easy	hard
4.	Number of cartons of milk the class needs for lunch today	easy	hard
5.	Number of children on the playground	easy	hard
6.	Number of children in our classroom	easy	hard
7.	Number of quarters in $3.50	easy	hard
8.	Number of hours you will be at school	easy	hard
9.	Number of cartons of milk the class needs for lunch tomorrow	easy	hard
10.	Number of shoes in our classroom	easy	hard
11.	Number of hot dogs you eat in a year	easy	hard
12.	Number of flowers in a field	easy	hard
13.	Number of grains of sand at the beach	easy	hard
14.	Number of pets our class owns	easy	hard
15.	Number of pennies in $1.00	easy	hard
16.	Number of squares we can see in our classroom	easy	hard
17.	Number of children in our classroom absent today	easy	hard
18.	Talk about your answers with your neighbor. Put an *X* by the ones you agree on.		

WARM-UP 7

Look for a *pattern.* Find the missing numbers.

1. 5, 10, 15, 20, _____, _____, _____

2. 21, 19, 17, 15, _____, _____, _____

3. 4, 8, 12, 16, _____, _____, _____

4. 42, 35, 28, 21, _____, _____, _____

5. If you have time, make up your own pattern problems.
   Give them to a friend to solve.

WARM-UP 8

1. Look for a *pattern.* Talk to a neighbor about the pattern you see.

2. Draw the next figure. How many small squares do you see?

3. Draw the next figure. How many small squares are there?

4. If you have time, draw your own pattern problem.
   Give it to a friend to solve.

WARM-UP 9

Get 24 square tiles all of the same size.

1. Can you put the tiles into 2 equal rows? _____
   Show your neighbor.

2. Can you put the tiles into 3 equal rows? _____
   Show your neighbor.

3. Try other numbers. Find some numbers that make
   equal rows. What are they? _____

4. Can 11 tiles be arranged in equal rows? _____

5. Can 14 tiles be arranged in equal rows? _____

6. Talk to your neighbor about problems 4 and 5.

WARM-UP 10

Get a pile of 36 counters.

1. Group the counters in some way so your
   friends can tell how many there are without
   counting by ones.
   Show your work to a neighbor.

2. Find other ways to group the counters.
   Show them to a neighbor.

3. Which way helped your neighbor tell the fastest?
   Draw a picture of your groups.

WARM-UP 11

You need a newspaper.

Find these things in the newspaper.
Loop them, and copy them down.

1. The price of something to eat

2. A street address

3. A phone number

4. A high and low temperature

5. The score of a game

6. The date of the paper

7. A number written in word form

Talk to a neighbor about where you found these things.

8. If you have time, find other examples of number information.

WARM-UP 12

1. *Estimate* the number of dots here.

2. A grid is added. There are 11 dots in the top left part.
    How does this information help you estimate the number of dots?
    Talk about your answer with a neighbor.

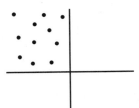

3. Now estimate again. _____

WARM-UP 13

1. What number does this picture model? _____

2. Subtract 15 from the model number.
   What number do you have? _____

3. Subtract 22 from the model number. What do you have? _____

4. Add 20 to the model number. What do you have? _____

5. Add 100 to the model number. What do you have? _____

6. Double the model number. What number do you have? _____

7. Add or subtract numbers you choose from the model number.
   Share with a neighbor.

WARM-UP 14

Name a fraction that comes between these number pairs.

1. 2 and 3 _____

2. 10 and 11 _____

3. 26 and 27 _____

4. 0 and 1 _____

Write fractions for these fraction names.

5. one half _____

6. two thirds _____

7. three fourths _____

8. four sixths _____

9. What other fractions could come between
   0 and 1? Name as many as you can.
   Talk to a neighbor about your fractions.

M

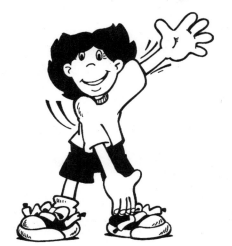

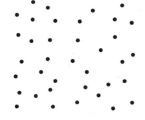

Answer the questions about the banks in the picture.
You may want to check your work with a calculator.

1. Which two banks contain 40¢ in all?

   _____ and _____

2. Which two banks contain 63¢ in all?

   _____ and _____

3. Which two banks contain 92¢ in all?

   _____ and _____

4. Which two banks contain $1.33 in all?

   _____ and _____

5. Which three banks contain $1.49 in all?

   _____, _____, and _____

6. Make up your own bank problems.
   Give them to a friend to solve.

1	3	= ?
5	7	= ?

‖   ‖
?   ?

1. Add across.
2. Add down.
3. Add your two across answers and write the sum in the top triangle. Add your down answers and write the sum in the bottom triangle.
4. What do you notice about your answers?

2	4	= ?
6	8	= ?

‖   ‖
?   ?

5. Add across.
6. Add down.
7. Add your answers across and down. Put these answers in the triangles.
8. What do you notice about your answers?

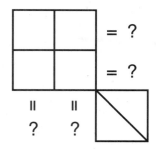

= ?

= ?

‖   ‖
?   ?

9. Make up your own puzzle. Use the same directions. Give it to a friend to solve.

WARM-UP 17

1.
$$\begin{array}{r} \boxed{2} \\ + \boxed{} \\ \hline \boxed{7} \end{array}$$

2.
$$\begin{array}{r} \boxed{5} \\ + \boxed{9} \\ \hline \boxed{} \end{array}$$

3.
$$\begin{array}{r} \boxed{7} \\ + \boxed{} \\ \hline \boxed{14} \end{array}$$

4.
$$\begin{array}{r} \boxed{} \\ + \boxed{} \\ \hline \boxed{0} \end{array}$$

5.
$$\begin{array}{r} \boxed{95} \\ + \boxed{} \\ \hline \boxed{95} \end{array}$$

6. Make up some of your own.

$$\begin{array}{r} \boxed{} \\ + \boxed{} \\ \hline \boxed{} \end{array}$$

$$\begin{array}{r} \boxed{} \\ + \boxed{} \\ \hline \boxed{} \end{array}$$

7.
$$\begin{array}{r} \boxed{10} \\ - \boxed{} \\ \hline \boxed{7} \end{array}$$

8.
$$\begin{array}{r} \boxed{} \\ - \boxed{6} \\ \hline \boxed{4} \end{array}$$

9.
$$\begin{array}{r} \boxed{} \\ - \boxed{5} \\ \hline \boxed{5} \end{array}$$

10.
$$\begin{array}{r} \boxed{10} \\ - \boxed{} \\ \hline \boxed{9} \end{array}$$

11.
$$\begin{array}{r} \boxed{10} \\ - \boxed{2} \\ \hline \boxed{} \end{array}$$

12. Make up some of your own. Use 10 in one of the boxes.

$$\begin{array}{r} \boxed{} \\ - \boxed{} \\ \hline \boxed{} \end{array}$$

$$\begin{array}{r} \boxed{} \\ - \boxed{} \\ \hline \boxed{} \end{array}$$

WARM-UP 18

Find the answers to these problems.

1. 5 more than 7 _____

2. 2 fewer than 12 _____

3. 4 more than 16 _____

4. double the amount of 15 _____

5. triple the amount of 3 _____

6. 13 more than 25 _____

7. 7 less than 39 _____

8. double the amount of 12 _____

9. 20 more than 45 _____

10. 30 less than 100 _____

Fill the blanks with numbers. Solve the problems.

11. _____ fewer than 14.   Answer _____

12. 50 more than _____.   Answer _____

13. double the amount of _____.   Answer _____

14. 100 more than _____.   Answer _____

15. If you have time, make up some problems of your own. Give them to a friend to solve.

WARM-UP 19

Here is a 2-floor A-frame and a 3-floor A-frame.

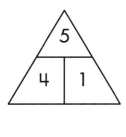
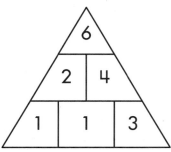

Finish these A-frames.

1.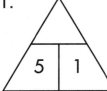

2.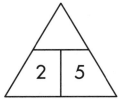

3.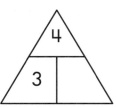

4.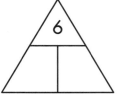

5.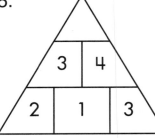

6.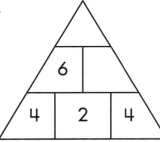

7.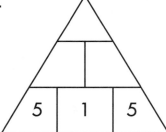

8.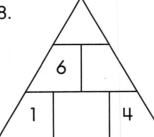

9.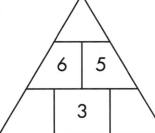

10.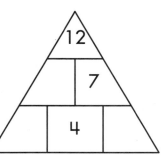

11. Make up some A-frame puzzles of your own.
Give them to a friend to solve.

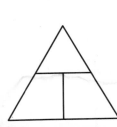
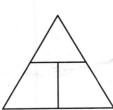
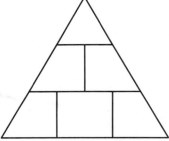
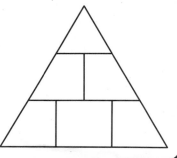

WARM-UP 20

1. Find ways to make 24¢. Finish the chart.

	Dimes	Nickels	Pennies
a.	2	0	4
b.	1	2	4
c.	1	1	_____
d.	1	0	_____
e.	0	4	_____
f.	0	_____	_____
g.	0	_____	_____
h.	0	_____	_____
i.	0	_____	_____

2. Use 4 coins. Make 17¢.

   _____ dimes _____ nickels _____ pennies

3. Use 6 coins. Make 23¢.

   _____ dimes _____ nickels _____ pennies

4. If you have time, make up a coin problem of your own. Give it to a friend to solve.

```
12   19   6   4
   17   21   11
 5   13   7   18
```

Use the numbers on the sign.

1. Find 2 numbers whose sum is 24. _____ _____

2. Find 2 numbers whose sum is 30. _____ _____

3. Find 2 numbers whose difference is 11. _____ _____

4. Find 2 numbers whose difference is 15. _____ _____

5. Find 2 numbers where one is two times, or twice, the other.

   _____ _____

6. Find 3 numbers that total 22. _____ _____ _____

7. Find 4 numbers that have the smallest total. _____ _____

   _____ _____

8. Write your own problems.
   Use the numbers on the sign.
   Give them to a friend to solve.

WARM-UP 22

1. I am a 2-digit number. Reverse, switch around, my digits to make a new number. Add me to the new number. The sum is 33.

   Who am I? _____

2. I am a 2-digit number. Reverse my digits to make a new number. Add me to the new number. The sum is 55.

   Who am I? _____
   Try to find another pair of numbers that works.

3. Make up a reversed digit problem of your own.
   Give it to a friend to solve.

WARM-UP 23

Solve these crazy problems.

1. 3 + 2 − 1 + 7 = _____

2. 30 − 10 + _____ = 25

3. 14 + 6 + 25 = _____

4. 2 x 10 = _____

5. _____ + 3 = 9

6. 10 + 10 + 10 + _____ = 30 + 8

7. 7 − 2 + 5 − 10 + 367 = _____

8. Make up some crazy problems of your own.
   Give them to a friend to solve.

WARM-UP 24

Put the +, − and = where they are needed. Make a loop around correct number sentences. You may use a number more than once. Find 5 subtraction problems.

```
11    6    4    4    8   ┌13    3    2
                        │ ║
 8    5    9    8    7   │ 6  + 7    1
                        └────────┘
16    8    5   15    9   14    7    9

 8   17   ( 4  =  2  +  2 )   9   10    7

 9   10    2    6    6   12    8    3

 3    4    8    4    3   ( 7  −  4  =  3 )

 3    6   10    5    5   11    6    5
```

WARM-UP 25

Put the +, −, × and = where they are needed. Make a loop around correct number sentences. You may use a number more than once. Find 5 subtraction and 5 multiplication problems.

```
11    8   ( 4  x  4  = 16 )  13    4    2

 8    5    9    8    7    6    7    2

16    8    6   15    9   14    6    8

 8   17    2    7    2   11   13    7
              ║
 9   13    7    6    6   12   15    5
         −
 3   14    2    2    2    7    4    3

 3    6    6   12    5   11    6    5
```

WARM-UP 26

The cost of 4 grapefruit is $1.00.

1. How much will 1 grapefruit cost?

2. How much will 2 grapefruit cost?

3. How much will 5 grapefruit cost?

4. How much will 8 grapefruit cost?

5. How much will 12 grapefruit cost?

6. How much will 40 grapefruit cost?

7. How would your answers be different if 4 grapefruit cost $2.00? Talk to a friend about your answer.

WARM-UP 27

Use the numbers 1, 4, 5, and 6 to make these problems. Place the numbers in the boxes. Each box should have a different number.

1. 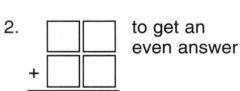 to get the greatest answer

2. to get an even answer

3. 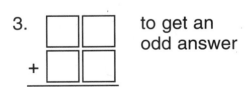 to get an odd answer

4. Write and solve your own box problems.

A word problem gives some facts and asks a question.

Look at the sample problem.
The facts you need to solve it are underlined.
Draw a loop around the question the problem asks.

<u>Diane has 15 toy cars.</u> <u>Karen has 17 toy cars.</u>
How many cars do they have in all?

For each problem
• underline the facts
• loop the question
• solve the problem

1. Mary had $15. She spent $9. How much money does she have left?

2. Tomas gave Eric three candy bars. Eric ate two of them. How many candy bars does Eric have now?

3. Is Yoko older than Roger? Yoko is 23 years old. Roger is 32 years old.

4. Carlos has 23 red pens, 18 green pens, and 13 black pens. How many pens does he have?

5. Larry has $18. He needs $20 to buy a new pair of shoes. How much more money does he need?

6. Last month Janice watched six nature shows, three cartoon shows, and twelve children's special shows. How many TV shows did she watch?

7. If you have time, make up some problems like these for a friend to solve.

Write a word problem to match each *headline* below.

Headline	My Word Problem

1. 17
  + 35
  52 toads	

2. 49
  − 15
  34 kites	

3. 152
  − 126
  26 cupcakes	

4. 25
  + 10
  35 snow days	

5. Make up a headline problem of your own.
    Have a friend write a word problem for it.

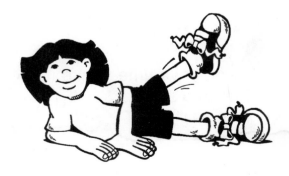

Some word problems give more facts than you need to solve the problem. Cross out the facts you don't need. Write the number sentence you would use to solve the problem. Solve the problem.

1. Kim had 16 pencils. Su had 5 pencils. Mark had 5 pencils and 4 pens. How many more pencils does Kim have than Su?

2. Marie bought a notebook for $3 and a pen for $2. She saw a computer game that cost $25. How much money did Marie spend?

3. José bought eight candy bars for $0.25 each. Marcy bought four candy bars for $0.20 each. How much money did Marcy spend?

4. Jo bought a kite that cost 5 dollars and some string that cost 2 dollars. She has 9 dollars in her bank. How much money did she spend?

5. Bill has 13 cats. Janya has 7 cats. Judy has 14 cats. How many cats do Bill and Judy have?

6. Make up a problem for a friend to solve. The problem should have information that is not needed.

Sometimes number facts are hidden as words in story problems. To solve these problems, you must first change the hidden fact from a word to a number.

Example

Jim has 8 pairs of shoes. He polished each shoe. How many shoes did he polish?
- The hidden number word is *pair.* It means 2.
- To answer the problem, you multiply 2 times 8 or add
  2 + 2 + 2 + 2 + 2 + 2 + 2 + 2.

Draw a loop around the hidden number word (or words) in these problems. Solve each problem. Label your answers.

1. Mindy had a dozen pencils. She gave 5 of them away. How many pencils did she have left?

2. Sonja has a quarter. Sandy has $0.30. How much more money does Sandy have than Sonja?

3. Sean drinks 4 glasses of milk a day. How many glasses of milk does he drink in a week?

4. Ann spent a quarter for candy and a dime for gum. How much money did she spend?

5. Sue wants to buy a book that costs $0.75. She has a half dollar. How much more money does she need to buy the book?

6. If you have time, write some fact story problems with hidden numbers for a friend to solve.

SMALL
10
CRAYONS
35¢

MED.
24
CRAYONS
60¢

LARGE
56
CRAYONS
90¢

Use the facts in the pictures above to solve these problems.

PROBLEMS   WORKSPACE

1. Leslie bought a small box and a large box of crayons. How much did Leslie spend?

2. Tom bought 34 crayons. He bought a medium box and a _____ box.

3. Ivan gave the clerk $0.50 for a box of crayons. He got a dime and a nickel in change. Which box of crayons did Ivan buy?

4. Kay and Rosa bought a large box to share. How much did each one spend?

5. If you have time, use the facts in the picture to make up some problems of your own. Give them to a friend to solve.

This table tells about a library book contest. Use the table to answer the questions below.

Name	Number of Books Read
Steve	5
Cathy	10
Val	8
Ahmad	11

1. How many books did Val and Cathy read altogether? _____

2. Which two people together read 13 books?

   _____ and _____

3. How many books did Ahmad and Steve read altogether? _____

4. Who read more books, Ahmad or Val? _____

   How many more? _____

5. Who read the most books? _____

6. Which pair read more books, Ahmad and Steve
   or Val and Cathy?

   _____ How many more? _____

7. Make up your own word problem to
   solve by using the table. Solve the
   problem or give it to a friend to solve.

Decide what number facts would be reasonable.
Fill in the facts. Solve the problems.

1. Omar ate _____ plums. Jerry ate _____ plums.
   How many more plums did Jerry eat than Omar?

2. John baked _____ dozen cookies.
   Carol baked _____ dozen cookies.
   How many dozen cookies did they bake in all?

3. Lucy bought _____ pencils at _____ cents each.
   How much did the pencils cost in all? _____

4. Sarah ate _____ pieces of pizza for lunch and _____ for dinner.
   How many pieces of pizza did she eat altogether?

5. Marcel bought _____ fish on Saturday for his fish tank.
   He bought _____ fish on Sunday.
   How many more fish did he buy on Sunday than Saturday?

6. If you have time, make up some problems with missing numbers
   for a friend to solve.

Hans and Lina went to the garden at 1:00 in the afternoon.
They looked for butterflies. They were surprised.
Butterflies are hard to find. They left at 3:00.
They had only found 5 black and yellow butterflies,
4 blue butterflies, and 7 white butterflies.

1. Why did Hans and Lina go to the garden?

2. How many butterflies did they find altogether?

3. Did they find more white butterflies or black and yellow
   butterflies? _____ How many more? _____

4. How many hours were they in the garden? _____

5. If they would have stayed in the garden for four hours, what time
   would it have been when they left? _____

6. If Hans and Lina had stayed in the garden until dinner time at
   6:30, how many hours would they have spent in the garden?
   _____

7. If they found twice as many of each kind of butterfly when they
   went to the garden the next day, how many of each kind would
   they find?

   black and yellow butterflies _____

   blue butterflies _____

   white butterflies _____

8. If you have time, make up a butterfly problem for a friend
   to solve.

Draw a picture to help you solve these problems.

1. You get on an elevator on the third floor of a ten-story building. The first floor is the ground floor.

   The elevator goes up to the top floor,
   then down 6 floors,
   then up 4 floors,
   then down 3 floors.
   You get off the elevator. What floor are you on?

2. You get on an elevator on the fifth floor of a twelve-story building.

   The elevator goes down 2 floors,
   then up to the top floor
   then down 7 floors,
   then up 5 floors.
   You get off the elevator. What floor are you on?

3. Talk to a friend about how you solved the problems. Do your answers agree? If not, talk about the problems and see if you can agree on the same answers.

Read these problems carefully. Fill in the blanks. Solve each problem. Label your answer.

1. Bob saw 93 _____.

    23 of them ran away.

    How many stayed?

2. Lee had 95 _____.

    She ate 23 of them.

    How many were left?

3. Jill paid 73 dollars for a _____.

    She paid 13 dollars for a _____.

    How much did she spend?

4. Rajiv has 116 _____ and 38 _____.

    How many animals in all does he have?

5. There are 78 _____ on a shelf.

    There are 96 _____ on the other shelf.

    How many are there in all?

6. Nancy collected 183 _____.

    Seven of them were broken.

    How many of them were not?

7. Write some word problems for a friend to finish and solve.

1. These are triangles.

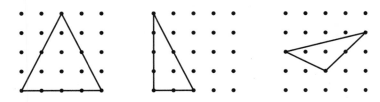

    Tell how they are alike.

2. Make other triangles. Make each one different in some way.
    Draw each one on a grid.

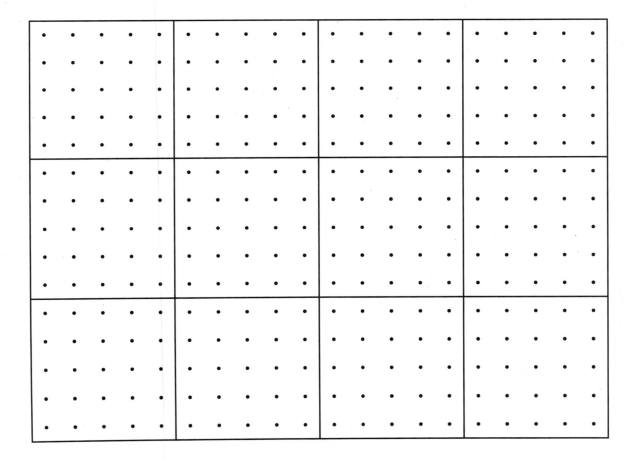

3. Talk to your neighbor about the triangles you drew.

WARM-UP 39

1. These are rectangles.   These are not rectangles.

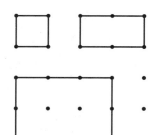   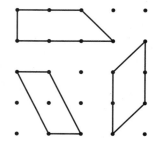

How are the rectangles alike?

2. Make other rectangles. Make each one different in some way.
    Draw each one on a grid.

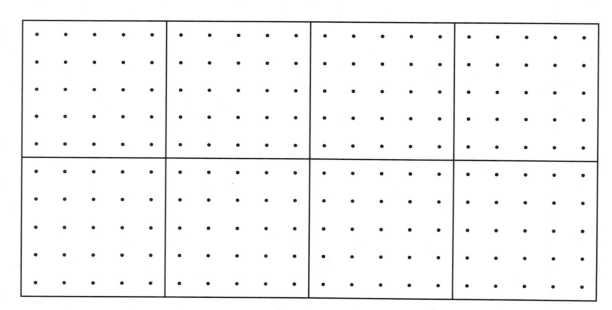

3. Talk to your neighbor about the rectangles you drew.

1. Find a line when you look at a table.

2. Find a line when you look at the doorway.

3. Where else do you see lines?

4. Describe the top of your desk.

5. Describe the outline of the door.

6. Describe the legs of your desk.

7. Describe the chalkboard.

8. Describe a globe.

9. Talk about these questions with your neighbor.

10. Practice drawing the box in the picture. It may help to trace it first. You can use a ruler to help you draw straight lines.

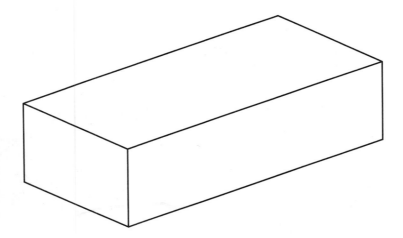

1. Look around the room.
   Find three objects that are in the shape of a *circle.*
   Write the names of the objects.

2. Find three objects that are in the shape of a *square.*
   Write the names of the objects.

3. Find three objects that are in the shape of a *triangle.*
   Write the names of the objects.

4. Find three objects that are in the shape of a *cube.*
   Write the names of the objects.

5. Trace this cube and draw some of your own.

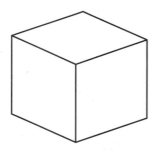

1. This shape is called a *hexagon.*
    Name 3 things that are true about this hexagon.

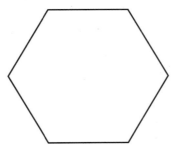

2. This shape is also called a hexagon.
    Name 3 things that are true about this hexagon.

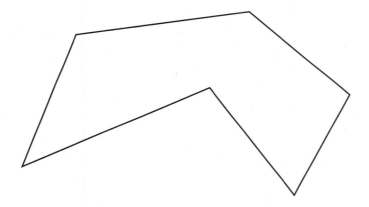

3. How are the two shapes the same?

4. How are the two shapes different?

5. Practice drawing hexagons of your own.

1. Place an *X* on the shapes you could make using only toothpicks.

2. Loop the shapes you would need string to complete.

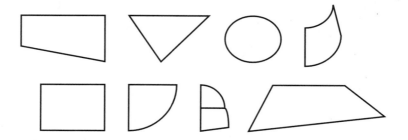

3. Do you know any of these shapes? What are their names?

4. Draw some shapes that you could make using only toothpicks.

5. Draw some shapes that you could make using only string.

WARM-UP 44

1. Look at the name of each shape. Draw them in the boxes. If you are not sure what shapes should look like, talk to your neighbors about them.

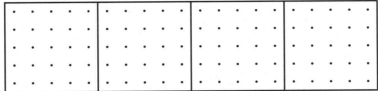

square   parallelogram   diamond   right triangle

trapezoid   rectangle   isosceles triangle   hexagon

2. Compare your drawings to the ones made by a friend. Discuss how they are alike and how they are different.

WARM-UP 45

M

1. Use only three toothpicks. Make as many letters of the alphabet as you can. Breaking toothpicks is not allowed.

2. Draw a picture of your toothpick letters.

3. If you have time, talk to a friend about how many triangles you see in your letters.

WARM-UP 46

Get a piece of one-inch graph paper from your teacher.

1. Draw these patterns on your graph paper.

2. Cut out the patterns. Fold them to make a cube.

3. Draw two more patterns that will each fold up to make a cube.
   They should be different from the patterns in problem 2.

WARM-UP 47

1. What does it mean that parallel lines never meet?
   Discuss your answer with your classmates and teacher.

2. Why do you think this figure is called a *parallelogram?*
   Find examples of parallel lines? Discuss your answer.

3. Draw two more figures that are parallelograms.
   Show your neighbor. Talk about why they are parallelograms.

WARM-UP 48

Get a square piece of paper.

1. How do you know it is a square? Tell your neighbor.

2. Fold your square into two triangles.

3. Make one more fold anywhere on your paper. Open the paper. Count the number of triangles.

4. What other shapes do you see? Trace all the shapes with your pencil.

WARM-UP 49

How many lines of *symmetry* are in these figures? Draw them.

1. triangle

2. rectangle

3. square

4. trapezoid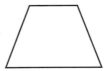

5. rhombus

6. circle

7. Talk to a friend about the circle.

WARM-UP 50

1. Take a sheet of paper. Roll it up. What shape have you made?

2. Name other things that look the same as this shape.

3. Look at the end of your rolled paper. What shape is it?
   Draw the shape.

4. Roll your sheet of paper the other direction.

5. Talk to your neighbor. Compare this shape with your first shape.

WARM-UP 51

1. Get three square tiles.
   Make as many different figures as you can by joining the squares whole edge to whole edge.
   Draw your figures on the back of your paper.

2. Do the same using four squares.
   Compare your figures to a friend's figures.

1. What is true about this picture? Loop the correct answer.

   A. *X* is heavier than *Y*.
   B. *Y* is heavier than *X*.
   C. *X* and *Y* are the same.

2. Draw a picture of the scale when *Y* is heavier than *X*.

3. If *X* weighed 16 ounces and *Y* weighed 1 pound, how would the scales look? Talk to your neighbor about this problem.

4. If *X* weighed 8 ounces and *Y* weighed 2 ounces, how many *Y*'s would be needed to balance one *X*?

5. How do you know which object is heavier? Talk to a friend about your answer.

M

Get a 12-inch or 1-foot ruler. How long is each line segment?

1. ————————————

2. ————————————————————

3. ——————————————————

4. ————————————————————————

5. ——————————————————————

Draw segments for these lengths.

6. 1 inch

7. 3 inches

8. $4\frac{1}{2}$ inches

9. $2\frac{1}{2}$ inches

10. Draw some line segments of your own. Give them to a friend to measure.

WARM-UP 54

Kate went fishing. She could keep only the fish that were greater than (>) 6 inches but less than (<) 14 inches.

1. Loop the lengths she could keep.

4 inch	20 inch	6 inch	8 inch	9 inch	10 inch
14 inch	11 inch	12 inch	13 inch	7 inch	18 inch
15 inch	9 inch	16 inch	17 inch	5 inch	3 inch

2. Kate did not have a ruler. What could she use to estimate the size of the fish?

3. How would the length of your little finger help?

4. How would the length of your foot help?

5. Kate caught a fish 20 inches long. How many inches too long was the fish?

6. If you have time, make some fish-length problems, and share them with your neighbor.

Each step Lin takes is equal to 2 feet. The front of the room was 12 steps long.

1. How many feet long is the front of the room?

2. Her mom's step is equal to 3 feet. How does this compare to Lin's step?

3. How many mom-size steps would it take to cross the room?

4. How many feet long is the front of the room?

5. How many yards long is the front of the room?

6. Tell your neighbor how you did these problems. You may work on the next problem by yourself or with a neighbor.

7. Now try dad-size steps.
   You decide how many feet long a dad-sized step should be.
   Write a new problem.
   Make sure you figure all the steps, feet, and yards.

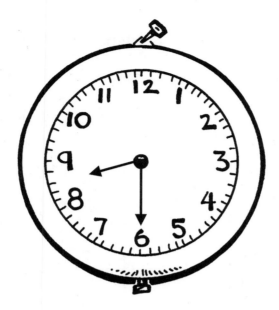

1. Here is a clock. Read and write the time.

2. What time is it 10 minutes later than the time on the clock?

3. What time is it one hour and 15 minutes after the time on the clock?

4. What are things that people might do in the morning at the time shown on the clock?

5. What are things that people might do in the evening at that time?

6. Draw a clock of your own showing the time school begins each morning.

7. If you have time, draw another clock and ask your neighbor to read the time on it.

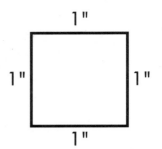

Each shape below can be made by putting 1-inch-by-1-inch square tiles together.

Find the perimeter and the area of each shape.

1.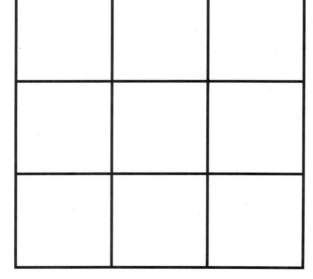

perimeter = _____ inches

area = _____ square inches

2.

perimeter = _____ inches

area = _____ square inches

3.

perimeter = _____ inches

area = _____ square inches

4. Draw your own shape with squares. Find its perimeter and area.

5. See if you can draw a shape that has a bigger area than perimeter.

WARM-UP 58

1. About how many feet high is the door of your classroom?
    Loop your answer.
    A. 1 foot   B. 7 feet   C. 12 feet   D. 36 feet

2. Loop the tool you would use to check your answer.
    A. ruler   B. yardstick   C. meter stick   D. scales

3. Name some things you would measure with a ruler.

4. Name some things you would measure with a yardstick or meter stick.

5. What would you use scales to measure?

6. Share your answers and ideas with a neighbor.

WARM-UP 59

M

1. If the width of the classroom door is about one yard and you use a ruler to measure it, the door would be about _____ feet wide. Use a ruler or yardstick to check your answer.

2. If a board is 24 inches long, it would be _____ feet long. Use a ruler to check your answer.

3. Tell a neighbor how inches, feet, and yards are related (are alike and different). Draw a picture to show your thinking.

4. If you have time, choose something in the room and measure it with a ruler or yardstick.

S	M	T	W	Th	F	S
		1	2	3	4	5
6	7	8	9	10	11	12
13	14	15	16	17	18	19
20	21	22	23	24	25	26
27	28	29	30	31		

1. What day is the 10th? _____

2. What date is the second Tuesday? _____

3. Loop the number of the day of your birthday.

4. Name the days of the week without looking. Practice writing them: Sunday, Monday, Tuesday, Wednesday, Thursday, Friday, and Saturday.

5. Which two days are weekend days? _____, _____

6. If Joe has hot lunch on Tuesdays and Thursdays, how many hot lunches will he eat this month? _____

7. Ask your neighbor a calendar question.

WARM-UP 61

1. If you have 1 quarter, 2 dimes, and 3 nickels, how much money do you have? _____

2. Write forty cents two different ways. _____, _____

3. How many cents is half of a dollar worth? _____

4. Your bank has at least two of each coin.
   You have pennies, nickels, dimes, quarters, and half dollars.
   If you shook two coins out, how much money could you get?
   How many answers could you get?
   Talk to your neighbor about all the answers you found.

5. If you have time, do the same problem shaking three coins out.

WARM-UP 62

1. Estimate the length of this crooked line in inches. I estimate _____ inches long.

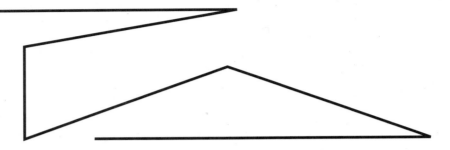

2. Get out a ruler to check your estimate. Talk to a friend about this problem.

3. On the back of this page, make up a crooked line problem of your own. Give it to a friend to solve. Your friend needs to make an estimate first. Then your friend can measure with a ruler.

   My friend's estimate is _____

WARM-UP 63

1. Find the perimeter of this polygon in centimeters.

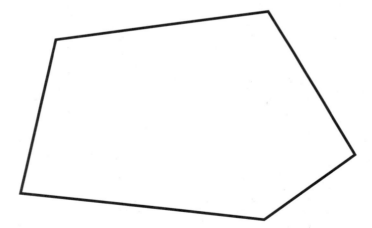

2. On the back of your paper draw a polygon of your choice. Make the perimeter about 20 centimeters.

3. Draw and measure other polygons.

1. If you were using a meter stick as a tool, what are some things you could measure.

2. When you measure something that is one meter long with just a little left over, what would you use to count the extra?
   Loop your answer.
   A. inches   B. feet   C. centimeters

3. Think of the size of a meter stick.
   Now think about how long 15 meters would be.
   How long would it take a dog to run to you if you were 15 meters away?
   Loop your answer.
   A. five seconds   B. five minutes   C. five hours

4. Name something that might take five minutes to travel 15 meters.

5. Talk with a neighbor about your answers.

1. Get 8 cube-shaped blocks from your teacher.
    Make a larger "cube" building.

2. Check your cube building with your neighbor's. Do all the faces
    look the same? _____

Talk to your neighbor about these questions.

3. How high is the cube? _____

4. How long is the cube? _____

5. How wide is the cube? _____

6. How many cubes are on the bottom layer? _____

7. How many cubes are on the top layer? _____

8. Study your building carefully. Draw a picture of your building.

9. If you have time, use the 8 blocks to
    build a different building. Draw it.

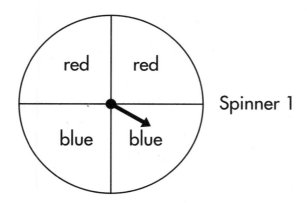

1. If you spin Spinner 1 _____ times, about how many reds would you expect to get?

2. If you spin it _____ times, about how many blues would you expect to get?

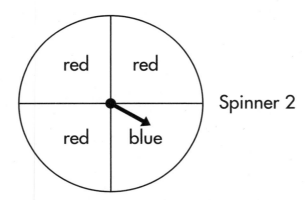

3. If you spin Spinner 2 _____ times, about how many reds would you expect to get?

4. If you spin it _____ times, about how many blues would you expect to get?

5. Make up a spinner problem of your own. Give it to a friend to solve.

Jon made sack lunches for a field trip.
He put a banana in one fourth of the lunches.

1. If you picked a lunch from a box holding all the lunches, how would you describe getting a lunch without a banana?

    A. never
    B. probably not
    C. maybe yes—maybe no
    D. probably
    E. always

2. If Jon packed 12 lunches, how many lunches did not get a banana? Draw a picture to help you find the best answer to loop.

    A. one fourth (3)
    B. one half (6)
    C. three fourths (9)

3. Talk to a neighbor about your picture. Compare your answers. What would happen if there were 20 total lunches for the class? How about 24 lunches? Draw new pictures to check your thinking.

WARM-UP 68

What is the chance of each of these events happening? In the space, write the letter of your answer choice.

A   B   C   D   E

(NEVER)   (PROBABLY NOT)   (MAYBE YES MAYBE NO)   (PROBABLY)   (ALWAYS)

1. You will grow another head. _____

2. You have a heart. _____

3. You will get a "tail" when you flip a coin. _____

4. You will get a "four" when you roll a die. _____

5. It will snow tomorrow. _____

6. You will ride the bus tomorrow. _____

7. You will take a space trip to the moon. _____

8. You will eat supper tonight. _____

9. You will see a live dinosaur at the zoo. _____

10. You will see a rainbow tomorrow. _____

11. Write five problems like these. Have a friend fill in the blanks.

1. Roll two number cubes.
   Add the numbers shown on the cubes.
   What is the highest sum you could get?

2. Roll two number cubes.
   Add the numbers shown on the cubes.
   What is the lowest sum you could get?

3. Roll two number cubes and add the numbers shown.
   List all the sums you could get.
   Talk to a friend about this problem.
   Come up with a plan to find all sums.
   You may want to make a list or a table to help you.

4. Now try some experiments rolling the number cubes.
   Keep a record of your results.
   Find out if any of the sums happen more often than others.

5. Talk to a friend about what happened and why.

1. Flip a penny. There are two ways it could land, heads or tails. Flip two pennies at the same time. How could they land?

2. Talk to your neighbor about this problem.
   Do both of you agree on your answer to question 1? _____.

3. Get two pennies from your teacher.

   If you flipped the two pennies 20 times, which one do you think would come up the most?
   heads, heads; heads, tails; or tails, tails?

4. Talk to your neighbor about your answer.

5. Test your idea. Record the results with tally marks.

Flip	Tally Marks
heads, heads	
tails, tails	
heads, tails	

6. Were you surprised? _____
   Compare your results with your neighbor.

7. Write down what you found out with this 2-penny experiment.

1. Choose two partners. Call yourselves A, B, and C.

2. You will be playing this game.
    On the count of three, each of you will show 1, 2, or 3 fingers on one hand.
    A gets 1 point if all three of you match.
    B gets 1 point if two people match.
    C gets 1 point if there are no matches.

3. If you play the game 20 times, who do you think will get the most points? _____ Talk to your partners about your answer.

4. Test your answer. Record the results with tally marks.

Player	Tally Marks
A (all three match)	
B (two match)	
C (no matches)	

5. Were you surprised? _____

6. If you have time, play another game of 20.
    Compare your results with the first game.
    Do you think this is a fair game?

    Talk to your partners.
    How were the results of the games alike?

    How were they different?

WARM-UP 72

You and your partner will need a deck of cards.

1. Take out the jokers. Shuffle the cards.

2. Turn ten cards faceup.

3. Count the red cards. Count the black cards.

4. Compare your results with another partner group.

5. If you shuffle the deck and start over, what do you think the first card will be when you turn it over? Loop your answer.

   A. red
   B. black
   C. an equal chance of getting red or black

6. If you turn over 10 more cards, how many black cards and red cards do you think will turn up?
   Try the experiment and record your results.

WARM-UP 73

You and your partner will need a deck of cards.

1. Take out the jokers. Shuffle the cards.

2. Turn ten cards faceup.

3. Count the face cards turned up. Count the number cards turned up.

4. Compare your results with another partner group.

5. If you turn a new card over, what do you think the next card will be? Circle an answer.

   A. a face card
   B. a number card
   C. an equal chance of getting a face card or number card

6. If you turn over 10 more cards, how many face cards and number cards do you think will turn up?
   Try the experiment and record your results.

WARM-UP 74

You will need a penny.

1. Flip the penny 20 times. Record the results with tally marks.

Flip	Tally Marks
heads	
tails	

2. Compare your results with a neighbor.

3. What is likely to happen on your next flip?
    Loop your answer.

    A. Heads will come up.
    B. Tails will come up.
    C. It is equally likely to be heads or tails.

4. If you have time, do the experiment again and compare
    your results.

WARM-UP 75

Scott flipped a coin three times. It came up heads three times.
He flipped the coin a fourth time.

1. What is he likely to get on the fourth flip of the coin?
    Loop your answer.

    A. Heads
    B. Tails
    C. It is equally likely to be heads or tails.

2. Talk to a neighbor about your answer and how you could test
    your idea.

3. If you use two coins and flip them at the same time,
    what are the possible head-and-tail combinations.
    Try it and record your results.
    First flip _____ , _____ ; Second flip _____ , _____

WARM-UP 76

M

1. There are only three blue blocks in a paper bag. Can you be sure what color block you will pull out? _____

2. Put a green block in the bag with the blue blocks. Can you be sure what color block you will pull out? _____

3. Put 3 green blocks in the bag with 7 blue blocks. Is one color more likely to be pulled out? _____

4. Talk to your neighbor about why you chose each of your answers.

5. Try a blocks-in-a-bag experiment of your own. Record your results.

WARM-UP 77

M

1. Take a sugar cube. Make a large *X* on 3 of the faces. Use a felt-tip marker.
2. Roll the cube 20 times. Tally the times an *X* comes up and the times a plain side comes up.

Roll	Tally Marks
X	
plain	

3. Talk to a neighbor about your answer.
4. What do you think will happen on your next roll? Loop your answer.
   A. *X* face will come up.
   B. Plain face will come up.
   C. It is equally likely to be *X* or plain.
5. What would happen if only 2 faces had an *X*? If you have time, try this experiment.

1. A paper bag contains an equal number of red jelly beans and green jelly beans. If you reach in the bag and take out one jelly bean, what color will it probably be? Loop an answer.

   A. It is more likely to be red.
   B. It is more likely to be green.
   C. It is just as likely to be red as green.

2. How could you test your answer without real candy?
Do the test six times and record your results.

3. Talk to a neighbor about the problem.
Did you get what you expected?
Try the test several more times.

WARM-UP 79

Jan bought a box of stickers at a yard sale. She knows that there are two times as many dull stickers as shiny stickers. She keeps them mixed together in the box.

1. She reaches in the box without looking and pulls out one sticker. What kind will it probably be? Loop your answer.

   A. Shiny
   B. Dull
   C. It is just as likely to be dull as shiny.

2. Talk to a neighbor about your answer.

3. How could you test your answer without real stickers?
Make a plan for a test. Do the test. Record the results.
Did you get what you expected?

WARM-UP 80

A class was asked which juice they liked better, orange juice or grape juice. This graph shows that 9 students liked orange juice and 6 students liked grape juice.

Juice Choices

orange	X	X	X	X	X	X	X	X	X
grape	X	X	X	X	X	X			

1. Did more children like orange juice or did more children like grape juice? _____

2. How many children altogether were asked what type of juice they liked? _____

3. How many more children liked orange juice better? _____

4. Did more than half or less than half of the class like grape juice? _____ Talk to your neighbor about how you figured out this problem.

5. Show what the graph would look like if three more children came to class and said they liked grape juice.

6. Now how many children altogether were asked what type of juice they liked? _____

7. Make up a question that can be answered using the graph. Give it to a friend to solve.

Paulo's Activities

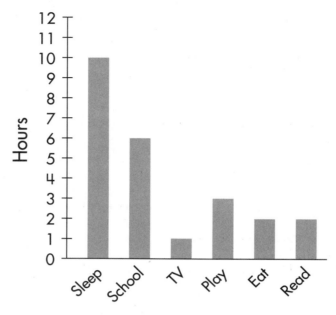

This graph shows how Paulo spent his day.

1. How much longer did Paulo sleep than eat?_____

2. How many hours all together did Paulo spend playing or watching TV? _____

3. How many hours all together did Paulo spend in school or reading?_____

4. Did Paulo spend more time sleeping or more time in school? _____

5. If Paulo had slept 2 more hours instead of reading, how many hours would he have slept? _____

6. Make up some questions of your own that can be answered with the graph. Give them to a friend to solve.

Finish the graph. Show the number of children that have each hobby. The line for reading is done for you.

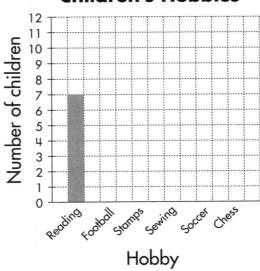

Children's Hobbies

Number of Children	Hobby
7	reading
10	football
2	stamp collecting
5	sewing
9	soccer
7	chess

1. Altogether, how many children play soccer or football? _____

2. How many more children like reading than stamp collecting? _____

3. Altogether, how many children were asked what hobbies they had? _____

4. Make up some questions of your own that can be answered using the graph. Give them to a friend to solve.

This line graph shows how many hot lunches were sold each day for one week.

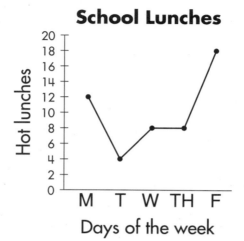

School Lunches

1. How many ate hot lunch on Monday? _____

2. On Wednesday, did more or fewer students eat hot lunch than on Monday? _____

3. Why do you think the line dropped down on Tuesday?

4. Why do you think the line went up on Friday?

5. The class had 20 students.
   The students who did not eat hot lunch ate cold lunch.
   On Monday, 12 ate hot lunch. How many ate cold lunch? _____

6. How many cold lunches were eaten each day for the rest of the week?
   Tues. _____ Wed. _____ Thurs. _____ Fri. _____

7. Get a colored pencil and draw dots on the same graph for the cold lunches. Connect the dots.

8. Talk to your neighbor about what this colored graph shows.

This graph shows which day of the week Mr. Dee's students prefer to watch TV. Each student had one vote.

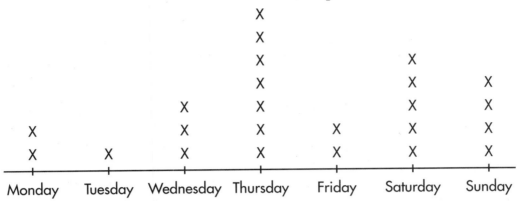

Favorite TV Day

1. How many students are in Mr. Dee's class? _____

2. Which day was the favorite to watch TV?

3. Which day had two less votes than Thursday?

4. How many students preferred the weekend? _____

5. Which days of the week tied?

6. How many students preferred school days ? _____

7. Make up some questions of your own for the graph. Give them to a friend to solve.

1. Get a grocery store advertisement from your teacher.
   What is the name of the grocery store? _____

2. Use the chart to tally each digit used in the prices of the items in
   the advertisement.

0	5
1	6
2	7
3	8
4	9

3. What digit was used the most? _____ the least? _____

4. Were your surprised about the digit that was used the most?
   _____ Talk to a neighbor about your findings.

5. Write down two things you found out about grocery store ads.
   Share these with a friend.

WARM-UP 86

Ms. Price's students sold tickets for the pet show. This bar graph shows the number of tickets they sold during one week.

Ticket Sales

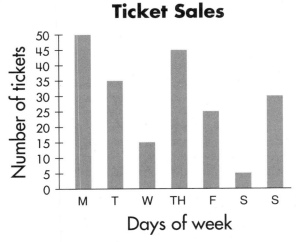

1. Write down everything you know from this graph.

WARM-UP 87

M

1. Choose a sentence in your reading book.

2. Count the number of *a*'s in the sentence.
   How many *b*'s are there?
   How many of other letters are used?
   Record how many times each letter appears.

3. Compare your findings with a neighbor.

4. Do you play games that ask you to guess letters? Which four letters would you want to guess first? _____,_____,
   _____, _____

5. Use different sentences from different kinds of books. Write about what you found.

WARM-UP 88

This is a *Venn diagram.* It shows how many students have dogs and/or cats. Each *X* stands for a student who has one or more of these pets.

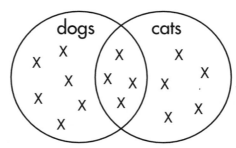

1. How many students just have dogs? _____
2. How many students just have cats? _____
3. How many have both? _____
4. Check your answers with a neighbor. Talk about what pet information this diagram does not tell us.

WARM-UP 89

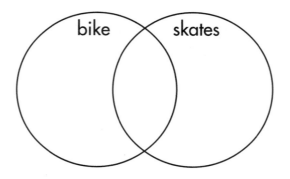

1. Fill in the Venn diagram to show that

   10 students owned only bikes.
   16 students owned only skates.
   7 students owned both a bike and skates.
   Use dots to show the information.

2. Make up a Venn diagram of your own. Tell what it shows.

WARM-UP 90

Ramon rolled a number cube for one minute. He rolled 9 ones, 10 twos, 7 threes, 9 fours, 8 fives, and 7 sixes.

1. Make a bar graph to show what he rolled. Finish labeling the graph. Put a title on the graph.

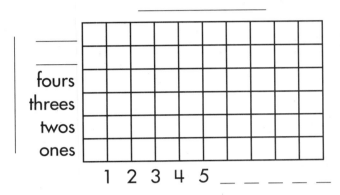

WARM-UP 91

Here is a circle graph.

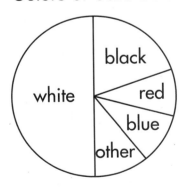

Colors of Cars Sold

1. What color of car sold the most? _____

2. What color was the second favorite? _____

3. Write down what else you understand from looking at this graph. Share your findings with a neighbor.

WARM-UP 92

1. This bar graph has parts missing. Think about what it could be showing.

2. Write a title on the graph. Write labels on the graph.

3. Could this graph be comparing other things? Check with your neighbor.

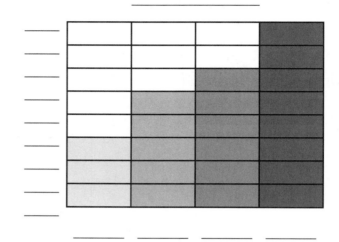

WARM-UP 93

$\boxed{M}$

1. Think of a question about pets. Write your question.

2. Ask six people your pet question. Record the data. Don't forget to include yourself.

3. Make a bar graph showing the data. Use graph paper and crayons. Be sure to label and title your graph.

4. What other survey questions would you like to ask the class?

WARM-UP 94

1. Make up stories that go with these number sentences.
    Share your stories with a neighbor.

    18 + 24 = 42

    17 − 4 = 13

2. 7 + 10 = 17. What is 7 + 20? _____

3. 14 + 20 = 34. What is 14 + 19? _____

4. 6 + 12 = 18. What is 36 + 12? _____

5. What is the best answer for $5.99 − $2.99? Why?
    A. about $7.00
    B. about $9.00
    C. about $3.00
    D. about $1.00

6. What is the best answer for
    298 + 199? Why?
    A. about 300
    B. about 400
    C. about 500
    D. about 4,000
    E. about 5,000

7. If you have time, make up a
    best-answer problem of your own.
    Give it to a friend to solve.

Triangles are worth 5 cents.
Circles are worth 4 cents.
Squares are worth 3 cents.

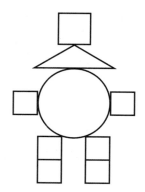

1. How much is this picture worth?

2. Make a picture worth 26¢.

3. Make a picture worth 33¢.

4. Make a picture. Have a friend figure out the cost. It cannot cost more than $1.00.

5. Talk to your friend about figuring out the cost of your picture.

WARM-UP 96

20¢ 20¢	25¢ 25¢	10¢ 10¢	5¢ 5¢	15¢ 15¢
squares	rectangles	circles	triangles	trapezoids

1. This shape picture costs 60¢.
    Tell your neighbor why.

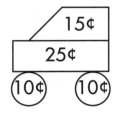

2. Draw a car or a truck that costs 70¢.

Draw shape pictures that cost

3. $1.00

4. 85¢

5. $1.25

6. $2.00

Solve the mystery problems. Use the clues. Make a guess.
Check the guess with the clues.

1. Clues
    - Ben has 2 more nickels than dimes.
    - He has 40 cents.
    - How many of each coin does Ben have?

2. Clues
    - Tammy has 4 coins.
    - She has 25 cents.
    - She has nickels and dimes.
    - How many of each coin does Tammy have?

3. Clues
    - Matt has 8 coins.
    - He has 35 cents.
    - How many of each coin does Matt have?

4. Make up some mystery problems
    using pennies, nickels, and dimes.
    Make up your own clues.
    Give them to a friend to solve.

Read the sentences and follow the directions.
If you cannot read a word, check with a neighbor.

You will need 4 different colors of paper.

1. Write *gallon* on one piece of paper.

2. Fold another piece of paper in half the fat way (not the skinny way). Unfold this paper and cut it on the fold line.
   Write *half-gallon* on each part.

3. Take another piece of paper. Fold it the fat way twice.
   There will be four parts when you unfold the paper.
   Cut it on the fold lines. Write *quart* on each part.

4. Use the last piece of paper. Fold it the fat way 3 times.
   There will be eight parts when you unfold the paper.
   Cut it on the fold lines. Write *pint* on each part.

5. Lee drank 2 pints, 1 quart, and 1 half-gallon of milk in one week.
   How can you prove he drank one gallon of milk?
   Use your paper pieces.

6. What are other ways to make a gallon?

7. The gallon piece equals one whole. Write the name of a fraction on each piece you cut out.

8. If you have time, write down some milk-drinking problems.
   Use the pieces you made.

WARM-UP 99

1. We both have pizzas of the same size. I cut my pizza into 4 equal pieces and you cut yours into 6 equal pieces. Who has bigger pieces? Draw pictures of the pizza slices on the circles to help you solve the problem.

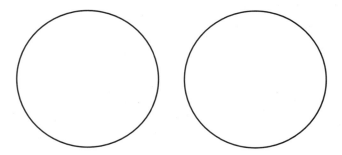

2. If I ate 3 pieces of my pizza and you ate 4 pieces of your pizza, who ate more pizza? _____

3. Would your answers be the same if the pizzas were different sizes? Talk to a neighbor about this problem.

WARM-UP 100

1. Draw a rectangle. Shade in $\frac{1}{2}$ of your rectangle.

2. Draw a circle. Shade in $\frac{1}{4}$ of your circle.

3. Draw a shape of your own. Shade in $\frac{3}{4}$ of your shape.

4. Make up your own shade-in problem. Give it to a friend to solve.

WARM-UP 101

Old McDonald raises ducks and cows.
The animals have a total of 9 heads and 26 legs.

1. How many ducks does Old McDonald have? _____

2. How many cows does Old McDonald have? _____

3. Make up a ducks and cows problem for a friend to solve.
    Make sure you know the answer.

WARM-UP 102

Use a list or chart to solve this problem.

1. Suppose you throw 3 darts. All of them hit the target.
    Complete the list to show all 10 ways to score.

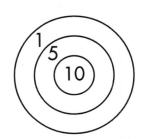

10	5	1	Total
✓✓✓			30
✓✓	✓		25
✓✓		✓	
✓	✓✓		

WARM-UP 103

1. Get 5 toothpicks. Make two triangles with 5 toothpicks.
    Draw these triangles.

2. Get 2 more toothpicks. Make 3 triangles with 7 toothpicks.
    Draw these triangles on the back of your paper.

3. Make 4 triangles with 9 toothpicks. Draw these triangles.

4. Each toothpick is worth 2 cents.
    How much do the triangles in question 3 cost?

5. Each triangle is worth 5 cents.
    How much do the triangles in question 3 cost?

WARM-UP 104

1. Cherry soda comes in six-packs.
    There are two six-packs to a carton.
    How many cans of soda would there be in 2 cartons?
    Draw a picture to help you solve the problem.
    Share your picture and your answer with a neighbor.

2. How many cans would there be in 3 cartons?
    Find the answer more than one way.

3. Make up a soda six-pack problem
    of your own.
    Share it with a neighbor.

WARM-UP 105

Amy threw 3 darts at the board. All of them hit the target.

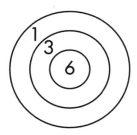

1. What are all the possible totals she could get?

2. Talk to a friend about how you solved the problem.

WARM-UP 106

1. Three children are at a party.
    Each of them shakes hands with everyone else only once.
    What is the total number of handshakes?
    Talk to a friend about how you solved this problem.

2. Now try this handshake problem with four children.

3. If you have time, figure out how many handshakes there will be
    at a party with five children.

WARM-UP 107

Look for a pattern. Find the missing numbers.

1. 1, 8, 15, 22, _____, _____, _____

2. 3, 8, 13, 18, _____, _____, _____

3. 24, 20, 16, 12, _____, _____, _____

4. 2, 4, 8, 16, _____, _____, _____

5. 1, 3, 6, 10, _____, _____, _____

6. If you have time, make up a pattern of
    your own and give it to a friend to solve.

WARM-UP 108

1. If you had 39 beans, how many piles of ten could you make with
    them? _____

2. How many piles of 5? _____

3. How many piles of 9? _____

4. How many piles of 11? _____
    How many beans would be leftover? _____

5. How many piles of 7? _____
    How many will there be leftover? _____

6. Decide how many beans you would like in each pile.
    Place the beans in the piles. Record the number of bean piles.
    Record how many beans are leftover.

TEACHER COMMENTARY AND ANSWERS

In some cases, space has been provided on the lessons where students can record their answers. In other cases, it is recommended that students use the back of the paper or consistently record answers in a math journal.

When a box with a check is found on the Warm-Up, check the italics print in this section.

It is assumed that students have access to calculators when they choose to use them.

Number Sense
WARM-UP 1

1. 13, 23, 32
2. 45, 54, 55
3. 229, 292, 922
4. 348, 384, 438
5. 345, 534, 543
6. $\frac{1}{4}$, $\frac{1}{2}$, $\frac{3}{4}$
7. 18
8. 100
9. 34
10. 176
11. 80
12. 416
13. 325
14. 50
15. 91
16. 110
17. 561
18. 272
19. 602
20. 439
21. Answers will vary

WARM-UP 2

1. a. <
   b. =
   c. <
   d. <
   e. =
   f. >
   g. >
   h. =
   i. =
   j. =
2. 963
3. 369
4. 872
5. 278
6. 35
7. 27
8. Answers will vary.

WARM-UP 3

1. 29
2. 50

3. 57

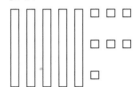

4. 147

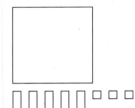

5. 235

6. Answers will vary.

WARM-UP 4

1. 12, 26, 40. Some students may continue shading in numbers beyond 40.
2. Even numbers should be shaded in.
3. Answers will vary. For example, students may write "even numbers," "every other number."
4. 15. Some students may continue shading in numbers beyond 30.
5. Multiples of 3 from 33–63 should be shaded in.
6. Answers will vary. For example, students may write, "every third number" or "multiples of 3."

WARM-UP 5

1. 14, 15, 16, 17, 18
2. 48, 49, 50, 51, 52
3. 97, 98, 99, 100, 101
4. 123, 124, 125, 126, 127
5. 205, 206, 207, 208, 209
6. 861, 862, 863, 864, 865
7. Answers will vary.
8. 12, 11, 10, 9, 8
9. 46, 45, 44, 43, 42
10. 95, 94, 93, 92, 91
11. 121, 120, 119, 118, 117
12. 203, 202, 201, 200, 199
13. 859, 858, 857, 856, 855
14. Answers will vary.

WARM-UP 6

Accept other answers for these problems, as long as they are supported by good reasoning.

1. easy
2. hard
3. Answers will vary.
4. easy
5. hard (Students move around!)
6. easy
7. easy
8. easy
9. Answers will vary.
10. easy
11. Answers will vary.
12. hard
13. hard
14. Answers will vary.
15. easy
16. Answers will vary.
17. easy

WARM-UP 7

1. 25, 30, 35
2. 13, 11, 9
3. 20, 24, 28
4. 14, 7, 0
5. Answers will vary.

WARM-UP 8

1. Answers will vary. Students may see that each picture is three greater than the one before.
2. The next figure should have 12 small squares (3-by-4).
3. The picture should show a rectangle that is made up of 15 squares (3-by-5).
4. Answers will vary.

WARM-UP 9

1. yes (2 rows of 12 tiles)
2. yes (3 rows of 8 tiles)
3. Answers will vary.
4. no
5. yes (2 rows of 7 tiles)

WARM-UP 10

Students may need help reading the long sentences.

1. Answers will vary. For example, 2 groups of 18 or 4 groups of 9.
2. Answers will vary.
3. Answers will vary. Students may have placed counters in 3 groups of 10 with 6 leftover.

WARM-UP 11

Answers will vary.

WARM-UP 12

Define estimate *for your students as making a reasonable guess. The estimate in the second question should be a better guess because there is more information to base the estimate on.*

1. Answers will vary, but the range will most likely be between 20 and 50.
2. Answers will vary, but students will probably say there will be 4 times more dots in the entire picture.
3. Answers will vary. There are actually 42 dots.

WARM-UP 13

1. 27
2. 12
3. 5
4. 47
5. 127
6. 54
7. Answers will vary.

WARM-UP 14

1. any fraction between 2 and 3
2. any fraction between 10 and 11
3. any fraction between 26 and 27
4. any fraction less than 1
5. $\frac{1}{2}$
6. $\frac{2}{3}$
7. $\frac{3}{4}$
8. $\frac{4}{6}$
9. Answers will vary.

Computation
WARM-UP 15

1. A and B
2. B and C
3. B and E
4. C and E
5. A, C, and D
6. Answers will vary.

WARM-UP 16

You will need to model this problem for students. The answer square should have the sum of the two numbers over it above the diagonal; the sum of the two numbers to the left will be below the diagonal.

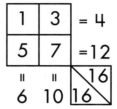

1. 4, 12
2. 6, 10
3. 16, 16
4. They both equal 16.
5. 6, 14
6. 8, 12
7. 20, 20
8. They both equal 20.
9. Answers will vary.

WARM-UP 17

1. 5
2. 14
3. 7
4. 0, 0
5. 0
6. Answers will vary.
7. 3
8. 10
9. 10
10. 1
11. 8
12. Answers will vary.

WARM-UP 18

1. 12
2. 10
3. 20
4. 30
5. 9
6. 38
7. 32
8. 24
9. 65
10. 70
11–15. Answers will vary.

WARM-UP 19

You will need to go over problem 1 and show that the number on top is the sum of the two numbers below. Note that in a 3-story A-frame, the middle number on the bottom floor is used for the sum of each number on the middle floor.

1. 6
2. 7
3. 1
4. Answers will vary, but sum of two numbers must be 6.
5. 7
6. 12 (top), 6 (middle)
7. 12 (top), 6 and 6 (middle)
8. 15 (top), 9 (middle), 5 (bottom)
9. 11 (top), 3 and 2 (bottom)
10. 5 (middle), 1 and 3 (bottom)
11. Answers will vary.

WARM-UP 20

1. c. 9
   d. 14
   e. 4
   f. 3, 9
   g. 2, 14
   h. 1, 19
   i. 0, 24
2. 1, 1, 2
3. 1, 2, 3
4. Answers will vary.

WARM-UP 21

1. 13 and 11; 18 and 6; or 19 and 5
2. 19 and 11; 18 and 12; or 17 and 13
3. 17 and 6; or 18 and 7
4. 19 and 4; or 21 and 6
5. 6 and 12
6. 6, 5, and 11; 12, 6, and 4; 13, 5, and 4; or 7, 11, and 4
7. 4, 5, 6, and 7
8. Answers will vary.

WARM-UP 22

Before you give this problem to your students, do the problem 34 + 43 = 77 on the board as an example.

1. 12 or 21
2. There are two possible answers. 23 or 32; 14 or 41
3. Answers will vary.

WARM-UP 23

1. 11
2. 5
3. 45
4. 20
5. 6
6. 8
7. 367
8. Answers will vary.

WARM-UP 24

Students may need help understanding the instructions.

The Warm-Up is easier than 25.

Answers will vary.

WARM-UP 25

Students may need help understanding the instructions.

The Warm-Up is harder than 24.

Answers will vary.

WARM-UP 26

1. $0.25
2. $0.50
3. $1.25
4. $2.00
5. $3.00
6. $10.00
7. Answers would double.

WARM-UP 27

1. Answers will vary, but the 6 and 5 must be in the tens place and the 4 and 1 in the units place.
2. Answers will vary, but make sure that the sum of the units digit is an even number.
3. Answers will vary, but make sure that the sum of the units digit is an odd number.
4. Answers will vary.

Word Problems
WARM-UP 28

You may want to work through the example problem.

How many cars do they have in all?

1. Mary had $15. She spent $9.
   How much money does she have left?
   $15 − $9 = $6.
2. Tomas gave Eric three candy bars. Eric ate two of them.
   How many candy bars does Eric have now?
   3 − 2 = 1
3. Is Yoko older than Roger?
   Yoko is 23 years old. Roger is 32 years old. No.
4. Carlos has 23 red pens, 18 green pens, and 13 black pens.
   How many pens does he have?
   23 + 18 + 13 = 54
5. Larry has $18. He needs $20 to buy a new pair of shoes.
   How much more money does he need?
   $20 − $18 = $2
6. Last month, Janice watched six nature shows, three cartoon shows, and twelve children's special shows.
   How many TV shows did she watch?
   6 + 3 + 12 = 21

WARM-UP 29

Answers will vary.

WARM-UP 30

1. Mark had 5 pencils and 4 pens.
   16 − 5 = 11
2. She saw a computer game that cost $25.
   $3 + $2 = $5
3. Jose bought eight candy bars for $0.25 each.
   4 × 20¢ = 80¢ or
   20¢ + 20¢ + 20¢ + 20¢ = 80¢
4. She has 9 dollars in her bank.
   $5 + $2 = $7.
5. Janya has 7 cats.
   13 + 14 = 27
6. Answers will vary.

WARM-UP 31

You may need to discuss the first problem and explain the concept of "hidden" numbers.

Example   pairs; 16 shoes
1. dozen   12 − 5 = 7 pencils
2. quarter $0.30 − $0.25 = $0.05
3. week   7 × 4 = 28 glasses or
   4 + 4 + 4 + 4 + 4 + 4 + 4 = 28
4. quarter dime
   $0.25 + $0.10 = $0.35
5. half-dollar
   $0.75 − $0.50 = $0.25

WARM-UP 32

1. $0.35 + $0.90 = $1.25
2. 34 − 24 = 10; small box
3. $0.50 − $0.15 = $0.35; small box
4. 45¢
5. Answers will vary.

WARM-UP 33

1. 18
2. Val and Steve
3. 16
4. 3
5. Ahmad
6. Cathy and Val, 2
7. Answers will vary.

WARM-UP 34

Answers will vary.

WARM-UP 35

Students may need help reading the long sentences.

1. Answers will vary, but students will most likely say, "to look for butterflies."
2. 16
3. white, 2
4. 2 hours
5. 5:00
6. $5\frac{1}{2}$
7. 10, 8, 14
8. Answers will vary.

WARM-UP 36

Discuss what is happening in the first problem and make sure students read the entire problem before they begin.

1. 5th floor
2. 10th floor

WARM-UP 37

1. 70
2. 72
3. $86
4. 154
5. 174
6. 176
7. Answers will vary.

Geometry
WARM-UP 38

1. Answers will vary. Students may say that they all have 3 sides.
2.–3. Answers will vary.

WARM-UP 39

1. Answers will vary. Students may give answers such as these: all figures have square corners, all figures have 4 sides, opposite sides are equal.
2.–3. Answers will vary.

WARM-UP 40

3. Answers will vary, but some possibilities are walls and windows.
4. Answers will vary.
5. Answers will vary, but students may describe the outline of the door as a rectangle.
6. Answers will vary.
7. Answers will vary, but students may describe the chalkboard as a rectangle.
8. Answers will vary, but students may describe the globe as being round or a sphere.

WARM-UP 41

Answers will vary.

WARM-UP 42

1. Answers will vary, but students may give answers such as, it has 6 sides and "corners," all the sides are the same length, it starts and stops at the same point, it is closed, it doesn't cave in.
2. Answers will vary, but students may give answers such as, it has 6 sides and "corners," the sides are different lengths, it "caves in," it starts and stops at the same point.
3. Answers will vary, but students may say that they have 6 sides and 6 "corners."
4. Answers will vary, but students may say that the sides are different lengths and that the second one "caves in."

WARM-UP 43

1. Students should place an *X* on all shapes that have straight sides.
2. Students should circle all shapes that have curves.
3. Answers will vary. Some possibilities are trapezoid, triangle, rectangle, circle, and quadrilateral.
4.–5. Answers will vary.

WARM-UP 44

This may be a hard problem for many students. You may choose to review vocabulary prior to giving this problem.

Answers will vary.

WARM-UP 45

Answers will vary. Possible letters are:
a c d f h k l n p t u y z

WARM-UP 46

3. Answers will vary. Here are some possibilities.

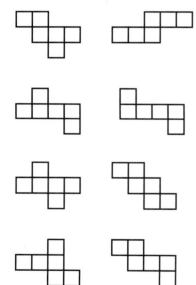

WARM-UP 47

1. Answers will vary, but students may say that the lines are the same distance apart and that they will never "meet."
2. Answers will vary, but students may see that opposite sides are parallel.
3. Answers will vary. *Check students' answers.*

WARM-UP 48

Answers will vary.

WARM-UP 49

1.

2.

3.

4.

5.

6.
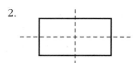

7. Answers will vary. *The students may see that there are an infinite number of lines of symmetry with the circle.*

WARM-UP 50

1. cylinder
2. Answers will vary.
3. circle
4. Answers will vary. *Students may say that it is the same shape but longer or fatter.*

WARM-UP 51

Students may need help reading the long sentences.

1. Answers will vary, but there are 2 basic shapes that can be rotated or flipped.

2. Answers will vary, but there are 5 basic shapes that can be rotated or flipped.

Measurement
WARM-UP 52

Students may need help reading the long sentences.

1. C
2. The *Y* side should tip downward.
3. The scales would be level.
4. 4
5. Answers will vary.

WARM-UP 53

1. 2 inches
2. 4 inches
3. 3 inches
4. $4\frac{1}{2}$ inches
5. $3\frac{1}{2}$ inches

6.–9. *Check students' work.*

WARM UP 54

1. 8 in. 9 in. 10 in. 11 in. 12 in. 13 in. 7 in. 9 in.
2. Answers will vary, but students might suggest the span of their hand, finger lengths, or fishing rod handle.
3.–4. Students should explain that knowing the length of their finger or foot may be compared to the fish length.
5. 6 inches
6. Answers will vary.

WARM-UP 55

1. 24 feet
2. Answers will vary, but students might suggest each mom step is one foot longer or her mom would take fewer steps to cross the room.
3. 8 steps
4. 24 feet *You may think it is a mistake to ask this question again, but look and listen for the students who make a connection between this problem and number one. This understanding is important to note.*
5. 8 yards
6. Discussion
7. Answers will vary.

WARM-UP 56

1. 8:30
2. 8:40
3. 9:45
4. Answers will vary, but students might suggest school beginning or breakfast.
5. Answers will vary, but students might suggest bedtime, bath, or storytime.

6.–7. *Check students' clocks.*

WARM-UP 57

1. 8 inches, 3 square inches
2. 10 inches, 6 square inches
3. 12 inches, 9 square inches
4. Answers will vary.
5. A five-by-five square would have a perimeter of 20 units and an area of 25 square units. *There are many other examples of rectangles with greater areas than perimeters. Enjoy finding them with your students.*

WARM-UP 58

1. 7 feet
2. A or B

3.–5. Answers will vary.

WARM-UP 59

1. 3
2. 2
3. Discussion about equivalent measurements—picture should show 3 feet equal to 1 yard and 12 inches equal to 1 foot.
4. Answers will vary.

WARM-UP 60

1. Thursday
2. the eighth
3. Answers will vary.
4. student practice
5. Saturday and Sunday
6. 10 hot lunches
7. Answers will vary.

WARM-UP 61

Students may need help reading the long sentences.

1. 60¢
2. $0.40 or 40¢
3. 50¢
4. Two-coin shake—15 answers:
   2¢, 6¢, 10¢, 11¢, 15¢, 20¢, 26¢, 30¢,
   35¢, 50¢, 51¢, 55¢, 60¢, 75¢, 100¢
   Three-coin shake—34 answers: 3¢,
   7¢, 11¢, 12¢, 15¢, 16¢, 20¢, 21¢,
   25¢, 27¢, 30¢, 31¢, 35¢, 36¢, 40¢,
   45¢, 51¢, 52¢, 55¢, 56¢, 60¢, 61¢,
   65¢, 70¢, 75¢, 76¢, 80¢, 85¢, 100¢,
   101¢, 105¢, 110¢, 125¢, 150¢

WARM-UP 62

1. Estimates will vary, *but look for reasonableness.*
2. 15 inches
3. Lengths and estimates will vary.

WARM-UP 63

1. 24 cm
2.–3. Answers will vary.
   Check students' work.

WARM-UP 64

Students may need help reading the long sentences.

1. Answers will vary. Examples: doors, chalkboards, or coatracks.
2. C
3. A
4. Answers will vary. Examples: a turtle or baby crawling

WARM-UP 65

1. Students build a 2-by-2-by-2 cube. *Make sure each face uses 4 blocks.*
2. yes
3. 2
4. 2
5. 2
6. 4
7. 4
8. Check the variety of ways students draw a cube.
9. Answers will vary. *Display the different shapes.*

Probability
WARM-UP 66

Before you give students this Warm-Up, fill in the space with 12, 40, or 100.

Students may need help reading the long sentences.

If you choose 12
1. 6 reds
2. 6 blues
3. 9 reds
4. 3 blues
5. Answers will vary.

If you choose 40
1. 20 reds
2. 20 blues
3. 30 reds
4. 10 blues
5. Answers will vary.

If you choose 100
1. 50 reds
2. 50 blues
3. 75 reds
4. 25 blues
5. Answers will vary.

WARM-UP 67

Students may need help reading the long sentences.

1. The best answer is "probably not," but accept "maybe yes— maybe no" also.
2. C
3. For 20 total lunches, 5 would have bananas and 15 would not. For 24 total lunches, 6 would have bananas and 18 would not.

WARM-UP 68

1. A
2. E
3. C
4. B or C
5. B or C
6. Answers will vary.
7. B
8. D or E
9. A
10. B, C, or D
11. Answers will vary.

WARM-UP 69

Students may need help reading the long sentences.

1. 12
2. 2
3. possible sums: 2, 3, 4, 5, 6, 7, 8, 9, 10, 11, 12
4. Answers will vary, but look for higher occurrences of 6, 7, 8.
5. Discussion. There are more ways of rolling the sums of 6, 7, and 8 with two number cubes.

WARM-UP 70

1. HH, HT, TT. Some students might say TH also.
3. Answers will vary, but look for students who realize that HT (or TH) will occur more often.
7. Students may discover that HT (or TH) occurs twice as many times as HH or TT.

WARM-UP 71

It may be helpful to tell students that this game is similar to rock, paper, scissors.

3. Answers will vary. Students may think they will be equal. In reality, two fingers matching occurs most often.
6. Answers will vary, but students should find that this is not a fair game.

WARM-UP 72

Students may need help reading the long sentences.

3.–4. Answers will vary.
5. C
6. About the same number of red and black, but specific answers will vary.

WARM-UP 73

3.–4. Answers will vary.
5. B
6. Probably more number cards, but specific answers will vary.

WARM-UP 74

1.–2. Answers will vary.
  3. C
  4. Answers will vary. *If time allows, collect all the data from the class and compare results.*

WARM-UP 75

1. C
3. The possible $\frac{4}{6}$ results would be: heads, heads; heads $\frac{2}{6}$ tails; and tails, tails.

WARM-UP 76

1. yes
2. No, because about one out of every four pulls would probably be green. *Students' wording will vary, but look for the idea that occasionally a green would be pulled.*
3. Blue is more likely to be pulled because there are more than twice as many blues.
5. Check the plan, the recordkeeping, and the results.

WARM-UP 77

2. Answers will vary.
4. C
5. Plain faces ( ) would occur more often than X faces ( ).

WARM-UP 78

1. C
2. Students might suggest using something else to represent the two colors. *Check the plan and recordkeeping.*
3. *If you have time, collect data from the entire class and display the results. The larger the sample, the closer the data will be to equal amounts.*

WARM-UP 79

1. B
3. *Check the plan, the record, and the results.*

Graphing and Statistics
WARM-UP 80

1. orange juice
2. 15 children
3. 3 more children
4. less than half
5. The graph would have two equal rows.
6. 18 children
7. Answers will vary.

WARM-UP 81

1. 8 hours
2. 4 hours
3. 8 hours
4. sleeping
5. 12 hours
6. Answers will vary.

WARM-UP 82

1. 19 children
2. 5 more children
3. 40 children
4. Questions and answers will vary.

WARM-UP 83

This might be a difficult problem for students who have never used a line graph.

1. 12 students
2. less
3. Possible answers may include the hot lunch was something many kids do not like. *Accept any reasonable answer.*
4. *Accept any reasonable answer.*
5. 8 students
6. 16, 12, 12, 2
7. *Check students' work.*
8. The colored graph shows how many cold lunches were eaten throughout the week.

WARM-UP 84

1. 24 students
2. Thursday
3. Saturday
4. 9 students
5. Monday and Friday
6. 15 students
7. Answers will vary.

WARM-UP 85

1.–4. Answers will vary.
  5. Answers will vary, but they

may find 9s, 5s, and 0s occur most often.

WARM-UP 86

1. Answers will vary. *It might be an interesting idea to collect all the class responses on a large chart so everyone can verify all the answers.*

WARM-UP 87

1 through 5. Answers will vary. *Students will probably find that vowels occur most often. The most frequent letters in English text in order are e, t, a, o, i, n, s, h, r*

WARM-UP 88

1. 6 students
2. 5 students
3. 4 students
4. Answers will vary. *Some may suggest other pets that students have are not included.*

WARM-UP 89

1.
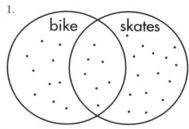

2. Answers will vary.

WARM-UP 90

Look for work similar to this example.

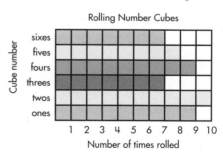

WARM-UP 91

1. White
2. Black
3. Answers will vary.

WARM-UP 92

Answers will vary. *Accept any reasonable answer.*

WARM-UP 93

Answers will vary.

Connections
WARM-UP 94

1. Answers will vary.
2. 27
3. 33
4. 48
5. C
6. C
7. Questions and answers will vary.

WARM-UP 95

1. 30¢
2.–4. Answers will vary.

WARM-UP 96

1. When all the costs for all the shapes are added together, the total is 60¢.
2.–6. Answers will vary.

WARM-UP 97

1. 2 dimes and 4 nickels
2. 3 nickels and 1 dime
3. 3 dimes and 5 pennies
4. Problems and answers will vary.

WARM-UP 98

You may want to make this a teacher-directed activity rather than an independent student activity.

5. *Students probably will lay cut-out pieces on top of a whole piece of paper to verify their thinking.*
6. Answers will vary. *Good time for class discussion.*
7. Write $\frac{1}{2}$ on half-gallon pieces.

   Write $\frac{1}{4}$ on the quart pieces.

   Write $\frac{1}{8}$ on the pint pieces.

WARM-UP 99

1. Mine would be larger (4 pieces).
2. I ate more ($\frac{3}{4}$ vs. $\frac{4}{6}$ pieces).
3. No. The size of the pizza makes a difference.

WARM-UP 100

1.

2.

3. Answers will vary. Check for accuracy.
4. Answers will vary. Check for accuracy.

WARM-UP 101

1. 5 ducks
2. 4 cows
3. Answers will vary. *Make sure students know the solution to their own problem before they share with another student. Sometimes there could be more than one right answer to students' problems.*

WARM-UP 102

1. *To get the class started, you may need to explain the list organization and model several examples. If this is the first time they have worked on such a problem, you may want students to work in groups or pairs.*

10	5	1	Total
√√√			30
√√	√		25
√√		√	21
√	√√		20
√		√√	12
√	√	√	16
	√√√		15
	√√	√	11
	√	√√	7
		√√√	3

WARM-UP 103

1.

2.

3.

4. 18¢
5. 45¢

WARM-UP 104

1. 24 sodas. Look for pictures of two groups with six in each. That picture should be doubled.
2. 36 sodas
3. Answers will vary. *An interesting discussion focused on the variety of methods for solving this type problem might be important to your whole class understanding.*

WARM-UP 105

You may want to encourage students to make a systematic list similar to WU102.

1. possible totals: 3, 5, 7, 8, 9, 10, 12, 13, 15, 18.

WARM-UP 106

This may be a difficult problem for students. Encourage them to draw pictures and act out the answers.

1. 3 handshakes
2. 6 handshakes
3. 10 handshakes. *Encourage students to make a chart and look for a pattern comparing the number of children to the handshakes. The answers are triangular numbers $\frac{n(n-1)}{2}$ where n is the number of children.*

WARM-UP 107

1. 29, 36, 43
2. 23, 28, 33
3. 8, 4, 0
4. 32, 64, 128
5. 15, 21, 28
6. Answers will vary. Check for accuracy.

WARM-UP 108

1. 3 piles of 10
2. 7 piles of 5
3. 4 piles of 9
4. 3 piles with 6 leftover
5. 5 piles with 4 leftover
6. Answers will vary. Check for accuracy.